Dear Readers,

welcome to this edition of our newly titled Martial Arts Magazine Australia. Unfortunately, we've encountered an unexpected challenge. Our Facebook page was recently hacked, and I've been actively working with Meta to regain control. As many of you know, our page served as a thriving community where we exchanged ideas, offered support, and built connections.

The page may still appear to be up and running, but unless you receive a direct message from me, we no longer have administrative control over it. To stay connected with us, we encourage you to visit and like our new page, "Martial Arts Magazine Australia."

Despite this setback, our magazine will continue to flourish here in Western Australia. I'm thrilled to share some outstanding articles contributed by individuals, both local and international. The spirit of community and dedication to martial arts that unites us remains strong. I am sure you will enjoy this edition of Martial Arts Magazine Australia (MAMA).

Thank you for your continued support and understanding as we navigate this unexpected challenge. Together, we'll overcome these obstacles and continue to foster the growth of our martial arts community.

Yours sincerely
Vanessa McKay

COPYRIGHT

All content published in MAMA (Marital Arts Magazine Australia), including articles, images, and other media, is the property of the magazine and is protected by copyright law. The author retains the copyright to their individual work, but by submitting their work to MAMA, they grant the magazine an exclusive, perpetual, and irrevocable license to publish and distribute their work in all formats, including print, digital, and online media. No part of MAMA may be reproduced, distributed, or transmitted in any form or by any means, including photocopying, recording, or other electronic or mechanical methods, without the prior written permission of the magazine.

MAMA respects the intellectual property rights of others and expects its contributors and readers to do the same. If you believe that your copyrighted work has been used in a way that constitutes copyright infringement, please contact MAMA immediately. Additionally, any use of MAMA trademarks, including the magazine's name and logo, without prior written authorization from the magazine, is prohibited.

MAMA strives to showcase original and unique content, and as such, does not accept any submissions that have been previously published or that are under consideration by other publications. By submitting their work to MAWA Magazine, the author confirms that their work is original and has not been published or submitted elsewhere.

In addition, MAMA reserves the right to edit all submissions for grammar, style, and clarity, and to reject any submission that does not adhere to the magazine's standards or guidelines. The magazine also reserves the right to remove or modify any content that is deemed inappropriate or offensive, at its sole discretion.

MAMA acknowledges and respects the rights of all individuals and groups and will not publish any content that promotes hate speech, discrimination, or any form of violence. The magazine also respects the privacy of its contributors and readers and will not share or sell any personal information to third parties without prior written consent.

By submitting their work to MAMA, the author agrees to abide by these copyright specifics and to grant the magazine the rights outlined in this statement. The author also certifies that their work is original and does not infringe on the rights of any third party. MAMA reserves the right to modify these copyright specifics at any time without prior notice.

If you have any questions or concerns regarding these copyright specifics, please contact MAMA at info@martialartsmagazineaustralia.com

TABLE OF CONTENTS

The International Muay Boran Academy	4
The Fundamental Principles to Practicing Tai Chi	7
Don't be a Frog	10
Fight Spur	15
Ask the Dojo Doctor	17
Yoga for the Martial Arts Body	19
New Beginnings with Aikido	21
Shihan Keiji Tomiyama	22
Early Shukokai Training Part II	28
Hard Ride	30
Seventy Lashes	31
The Place of Traditional Karate in the Modern Martial Arts Landscape	34
How Karate Saved My Life	39
Watching the Tree	41
Possibilities	46
South West Goju-Ryu Karate-do Assoc Inc WA	50

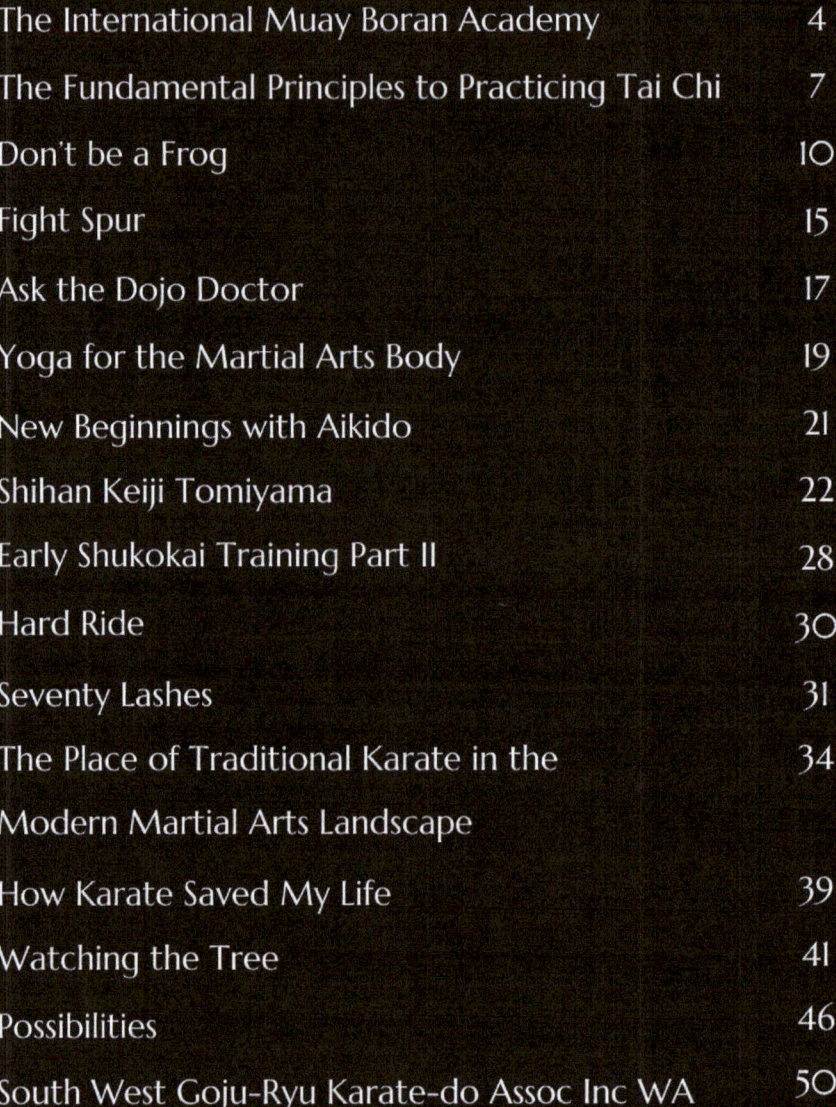

Image by Veronika Ryabova

Master Marco De Ceraris

IMBA

The International Muay Boran Academy

The International Muay Boran Academy (IMBA) is the first international school devoted to the development of traditional Thai unarmed fighting disciplines (since 1993). IMBA has been created thanks to the dedication of one of the most renowned worldwide exponents of Muay Thai, the Italian Master Marco De Cesaris, founder and technical director of IMBA.

In the last few years, the International Muay Boran Academy has successfully created a global network of highly qualified Muay Thai Boran instructors in Europe, Latin America and Oceania. Over the past 20 years, the International Academy founded by Master Marco De Cesaris, has concentrated all its efforts on the re-organisation and dissemination of Thailand's forgotten unarmed combat techniques. The conventional name chosen to denote this ancient martial discipline was Muay Thai Boran; a set of forgotten techniques designed over the centuries by the Kingdom of Siam's masters.

Muay Thai Boran as it is practised in all IMBA Branches worldwide is fully combat oriented: its main goal is making men and women ready for all-out fighting. For this reason, all IMBA members are welcome to take part in technical seminars held regularly; advanced seminars are devoted to the deeper understandings of ancient fighting techniques and strategies (i.e., Mae Mai-Look Mai Muay Thai, Chern Muay, Kon Muay Kae) and their combative applications with a special attention on their use in self-defence.

Open courses for instructors are frequently staged both locally and internationally, and Khan grading sessions for students and instructors are held regularly. IMBA Muay Boran is a complete fighting art that combines the ring fighting science of Muay Thai with the martial applications of ancient Siamese unarmed combat techniques. In encouraging the two different aspects of the art to coexist, IMBA Muay Boran successfully bridges the gap between modern combat sports and traditional martial arts.

Thanks to the effort of all IMBA members worldwide, traditional Muay has finally become a true world heritage, as advocated by the Thai masters of old time.

Combat Muay Boran (the most combative interpretation of the original unarmed Thai martial arts' fighting skills), IMBA Lert Rit (a Siamese military Close Combat style adapted to civilian use) and IMBA Muay Pram (the present-day version of classical Thai Grappling) represent the three technical pillars of IMBA Muay Boran, the modern and scientific version of original Muay Thai Boran, developed since 2005.

Master Marco has been a Muay Thai practitioner since 1978 and has been certified as a teacher of Muay by the Ministry of Education of Thailand (in 1991). During his career, he was an athlete, coach of professional Thai boxers, judge / referee, promoter and founder of the first Italian Muay Thai Federation. In the year 2007, he was awarded the Gold Medal in the World Muay Boran Championships, solo Technical Forms competition, held at Bangkok National Stadium. In 2012, he was awarded the 15th Khan of Muay Thai Boran (and the title of Bramarjarn or Grand Master of the Art) and the Gold Mongkon by the Governor of Ayutthaya Province, Thailand.

IMBA is in its novice stages of introducing its curriculum to Australia. Classes have commenced in Perth and are looking to extend to all states.

For further information on classes please contact:
Australian Representative: Kru Maria Quaglia at imbaaust@gmail.com.au .
Website: www.muaythai.it
YouTube: https://youtube.com/@MuaythaiIt?si=cOeBshBP9AzuBQwo

Kru Maria Quaglia with Master Marco

Fundamental Principles to Practicing Tai Chi.

In the previous article, we discussed broadly what Tai Chi is and what Tai Chi can do for you. Now that we have a bit of a deeper understanding of the benefits Tai Chi offers, let us now look at a few essential principles that need to be applied when starting any Tai Chi program.

To gain all the benefits and understand Tai Chi in all its glory, takes time, dedication, patience and consistency with your practice. As a beginner, you may expect to achieve your goals in your very first lesson. It should be understood that the chances of this happening are unlikely and that you should not let it deter you from practicing. Tai Chi is a deep and multi-faceted art that requires practice to achieve your desired objectives. However, if you can understand and apply some of the following principles, you can expect to reach your goals sooner.

Rising to the top

This refers to your spirit. When performing Tai Chi movements, keep your head upright, firm but relaxed. Do not allow tension to come in, as this will block the flow of energy. The best way to gauge the correct technique is to look where your eye line level is. Try not to look down at your toes or higher than your head. When you rise your spirit to the top, you will attain a state of mental freshness.

Lower the chest, raise the back

A simple way to practice this principle is to think of caving in your chest and rounding your shoulders forward while keeping your back straight. Just be mindful to keep your body relaxed without any tension. Again, this will allow the energy to flow more freely throughout your body.

Loosen the waist

All your movements are driven from the waist, which is the controlling part of the torso. Keeping your waist supple will relax the upper body movements while maintaining a strong stable stance.

Differentiate 'Apparent' and 'Solid'

When you place all your body weight on one leg (solid) and counter support your balance with the leg that has no body weight on it (apparent), you will have a better understanding of how to make your movements more agile when stepping.

Sink shoulders, drop elbows

To understand this feeling, stand upright and imagine hugging an invisible beach ball against your chest. Now, if your shoulders are tense and your elbows are high, simply exhale slowly and watch how they sink. Notice how your upper body suddenly becomes more relaxed.

Use will, not strength

One way to interpret this is to let your mind be focused and concentrate on the movements to come out as naturally as possible without forcing it. Again, the aim here is to get your body to relax using the power of the mind.

Coordination between top and bottom

An easy way to think of this is to make sure that your upper body movements are coordinated with your lower body. Not just hands and feet, but also the waist, shoulders, torso. Even the eyes and breathing must be unified together so that they all start moving together and finish moving together for any given move. This is the essence of 'Yin-Yang harmony'.

Internal and external unity
Again, we look at the concept of yin-yang theory applying to movements between the mind and the body. Essentially, if your movement is extended or 'open', then so should your mind be. Likewise, if your movement is drawn in, your mind should be 'closed' or more focused.

Continuity without break
When performing a set of combined movements of a Tai Chi routine, each and every individual move should link to each other as if they were one long continuous movement rather than many separate ones.

Seeking stillness in movement
When you slow movements down, your breathing will naturally become deep and long. The body is more relaxed and then there will be no blockages to allow the energy to flow freely throughout the body. The slower the movements, the better, almost to the point where it feels as if you are not moving at all.

Applying these principles is one of the first steps to your success in Tai Chi practice. You may also come across some styles of Tai Chi that may look different in their movements (we will discuss this in another article) but all of them should share these essential principles. One of the main purposes in the correct use of the fundamentals is to help the practitioner cultivate what is known as 'chi' energy, which can be considered the life force that helps regulate our well-being.

https://www.perthtaichiacademy.com

Image Sergey Nivens

"The frog at the bottom of the well will never know the eternity of the sky."

I'd like to discuss karate's 'bigger picture'. That karate is larger than any one group, style, teacher, or nationality. I want to open up the box of knowledge and information marked "Suitable for 'my' style only" and put forward the crazy idea that good karate is good karate regardless of the branding and tribal thinking the art has suffered from since going global. I also want to balance that idea by looking at 'bad karate' and why those who practice it don't need me or anyone else to highlight just how bad they really are.

An old Chinese proverb points to something so obvious its message is often lost on those who come across it,
"The frog at the bottom of the well will never know the enormity of the sky."

So here's the thing, we are all in danger of being a frog. If you sit at the bottom of your well (style, club, association) safe in the belief that you are looking up at the entire sky your chances of understanding the enormity of karate (or any martial art) is limited, actually it is impossible. When you draw all your knowledge and information from a single source (teacher, association, style), then you are merely copying the actions of another frog sitting at the bottom of a different well. Because no single source of information, however famous or well promoted, will help you find what you've been telling yourself you're searching for.

But wait a minute. If you don't stick to a single school of karate, teacher, or organisation, then learning karate would become chaotic, right? It would stop making sense, wouldn't it? HELLO! Just look around you. Most of today's karate makes no sense at all! Sport and business masquerading as budo, self-defence being taught by people who have never had a serious fight in their life, and money and commerce taking the place of morals and personal growth. If that doesn't look like nonsense to you then turn the page now and read the next article, because nothing I'm talking about here will mean a thing. But before I go any further, I want to address something we all have to guard against…the duality of thought. Its a problem for people when confronted by it, few can say with any degree of honesty that we are impervious to it.

By duality of thought, I mean the ability to believe you are doing one thing yet act contrary to that belief and not see a problem living with the difference. In learned circles, the notion of 'Cognitive Dissonance' goes someway to explaining the forces at play here. The discomfort felt by an inability to align your thoughts with your actions causes you to suspend your normal clarity of thought and accommodate your good thought and bad action as being equally okay. Here are a few classic examples of what I mean…

Karate-do is about polishing your spirit.
Well, it might be, but if that's what you believe, then why have you turned it into a job? If the aim of your karate is to "polish your spirit", how did you come to be so dependent on your students for your income? How come you spend very little time training (polishing) compared to teaching (pampering to your ego)? If you don't have clear answers to questions like these then it's safe to say your relationship with your martial art is dualistic.

If your home life and personal relationships are problematic, how exactly is climbing into your do-gi and wrapping a belt around your hips helping you with that? If your karate comes on and off like your shoes, which part of your training is making your life a better experience? If you hate your job, why haven't you found ways to solve that situation from lessons learnt during training?

You can't focus inward on yourself (polish your spirit) if most of your involvement with karate is spent focussing outward on others. Any martial practice that uses the suffix 'do' points to a way of being in the world. However, if you suffer from dualistic thinking, then it's hard to know where you are, other than lost. Here's another example….

Karate is an art of self-defence
Well again, it might be, but not for you. Not if you're unable to defend yourself from your own ego or the adversities life brings your way. If all you have are a few kicks and punches and a couple of remembered kata, then, in reality, you don't have much of a defence at all, regardless of what you believe. The dream of being able to defeat the bad guy in the street or the intruder in your home is a powerful one. No one wants to be taken advantage of that way. But the vast majority of people training in the martial arts, especially those deemed 'traditional', will never face these situations, and it's exactly those odds that allow the martial arts to be sold as a means of physical self-protection… because the chances are, you'll never find out that your training was useless.

As to the stories of those who have fought the good fight and won. In 50 years of training I've heard the story many times but have yet to meet a single person who has faced such a situation and walked away unscathed due to their superior fighting abilities. In truth, if you don't have the mentality to fight, knowing a few 'moves' won't help you. As well as the 'fight or flight' most are familiar with, there are also the 'freeze and appease' responses.

When faced with a surprise attack or potentially overwhelming situation, people with no place to run and an unwillingness to fight (fight or flight) will either freeze or attempt to appease their adversary. Either option denies you an opportunity to take the initiative and solve the situation to your advantage. I doubt the majority of instructors teaching 'practical self-defence' have trained in, let alone mastered, the mindset required to handle raw and unforgiving violence. If you advertise self-defence as a part of your training, I hope you're honest enough with your customers to tell them everything your teaching them is theoretical.

In nature, few things happen overnight. So, the seismic shift in thinking over the past sixty or so years has, by steady increments, changed how today's karateka think about their training. No longer the brutally effective fighting system it once was, or the severe self-effacing practice it turned into when the notion of 'jitsu' was replaced by 'do'. Karate today is not by any measure what it used to be. That said, the comparison between the past and the present would have little meaning if it were not for the current crop of karate instructors relying so heavily on the past to validate their 'modern' approach to training.

If your involvement with karate is dependent on teaching others then from my perspective you're lost. Regardless of your (good) intentions, when your focus shifted away from your own personal cultivation and onto teaching others, your notion of 'do' and 'self-defence' was severely compromised by your decision. The recent Covid-19 situation highlighted this mistake to a great many martial arts instructors around the world, impacting their lives (through loss of income) in a far more significant way than was necessary. If only they had understood how to defend themselves financially as well as physically. Although I doubt the idea of teaching karate as a job will die out completely, the recent lock-down may have provided some 'instructors' with an opportunity to spot their error in judgment and recalibrate their relationship with karate. In truth, that would take a willingness to be open to personal introspection and have the courage to act. Sadly, not so many instructors teaching karate these days have either in sufficient quantity to be of any use.

The final example of dualistic thinking I'll provide is found in the idea of 'Family'. You'll hear this word used a lot in karate circles. It's a nice, wholesome thought, but it's also a deep-seated illusion in the mind of many modern karateka. I highlighted its origins in my previous article (WAMA #1) so please refer to that edition if you'd like to know more.

Our dojo/group/world-wide association is like a family
Except that's not really true, is it? Parents help their offspring when they're facing hardship. They provide support, both emotional and financial. The myth of the 'karate family' was well and truly tested during the Covid-19 pandemic. I'm unaware of any 'professional' instructor, group, or organisation that offered more than a few classes online to tide folk over the lock-downs. With all the money that flows into these 'families' year after year, if ever there was a time for that flow to go the other way, it was during the pandemic.

Students and their families faced real hardship, loss of income, and, in some cases the loss of their homes. So where was the parent then? How many associations offered financial assistance to their members? How many so called 'sensei' gave back to their students in a meaningful way. Not as many as those who reminded their followers constantly to stay 'loyal' and to get back to training as soon as they could. And before you ask, all the students at my dojo were offered, no strings attached, no payback, financial assistance. Only one had to make use of it. The two-way street of loyalty is in practice, more likely to be a one-way road leading to the best interests of the instructor and the group. Clearly visible from a distance, the notion of family for a great many training in karate these days is more closely aligned to the activities of a cult than a clan.

Taking responsibility
When you're a frog at the bottom of a well, your chances of comprehending the enormity of the sky is non-existent. You simply can't know what you don't know. When you're a karateka with a narrow view of karate, your chances of grasping the enormity of the art are restricted in similar fashion. The notion of 'Shoshin', the 'Beginner's mind', or more appropriately ones 'First mind', is key to escaping the claustrophobic confines of your situation at the bottom of the well. Shoshin reflects an openness, curiosity, and daring. An inquiring mind hungry to understand new things and expand its horizons. To go deeper and move beyond the superficial. Now, contrast that with the narrow message coming from so many karate instructors today who push the idea that above all else you have to be a loyal follower. When you do that you begin to understand how dualistic thinking stifles potential and transforms so many enthusiastic karateka into nothing more than frogs sitting at the bottom of their own myopic well.

Books by Mike Clarke are available where all good books are sold.

Fight Spur

by Chia Zhi Jie

This karate school doesn't have tests or gradings.

When one thinks of a karate class, the picture that comes to mind is usually a group of kids with a plethora of belt colours, maybe even a few black belts, standing in neat rows, shouting as they throw punches.

Karate in this day and age has gained a somewhat negative impression. It is known as something kids do for a few years, get a black belt and move on to other, more contact heavy martial arts.

Zhi Jie grew up in that environment. His parents enrolled him into a karate class at the local community centre when he was a kid. He was inspired by the vision of elevating karate's reputation to rival the stereotypical "tough and effective" image that Muay Thai, Boxing and Kickboxing has. His goal was to capitalise sport karate's evasiveness and footwork by importing aspects of boxing and kickboxing to make the style practical. Despite having a background in Go-Ju Ryu, he drew very little from that school, instead drawing from his experience as a competitor in sport kumite and amateur kickboxing.

The belt system in FightSpur differs from what you'd typically find in traditional karate organisations. In traditional karate, a first-degree black belt denotes "basic competency", in which a student has learnt the fundamentals and is now ready to pursue advanced training.

At FightSpur, this level of skill is represented by the blue belt. Black belts in FightSpur denote a much higher level of technical and practical skill.

Promotions are based solely on performance and competency; they do not have tests or gradings. Instead, instructors monitor the students' progress and promote them once they reach the required proficiency. Students can earn 4 stripes on each belt before being promoted to the next belt. Stripes on a black belt represent the degrees (1 to 5).

FightSpur is a karate school in Singapore that combines the core principles of sport karate, kickboxing and full contact karate, creating an effective and efficient system geared towards self-defence and competitive fighting. It incorporates sport karate's long range attacks, distance control, timing and footwork, with kickboxing's long combinations, short range attacks and conditioning. This is a martial art designed to impart effective skills, and is applicable in both full contact and sport karate competitions.

We routinely compete in both Karate and Kickboxing competitions.

Follow us on:
Instagram: https://instagram.com/fightspur_karate/
TikTok: https://www.tiktok.com/@fightspurkarate
Linkedin: https://linkedin.com/company/fightspur
YouTube: https://youtube.com/@fightspur
Facebook: http://fb.me/FightSpur.Karate

The Dojo Doctor Answers Your Tricky Training Related Questions.

I started training with a friend of mine and at first it was great we were both learning together, but I have started to take my journey more seriously. I want to grade up the ranks and maybe teach someday. He on the other hand, is happy to slack off and talk through training. It annoys me and I am afraid it will ruin our friendship.

Dear Martial Artist, I understand your concern, and it's a situation that many martial artists encounter during their journey. Balancing friendship with the pursuit of personal goals in martial arts can be challenging. Here are some steps you can consider:

Open Communication: Sit down with your friend and have an open, honest conversation about your respective goals and expectations. Express your passion for martial arts and your desire to advance, possibly to a teaching level. Ensure your friend understands the importance of your commitment.

Set Boundaries: Establish training boundaries together. Let your friend know that when it's time to train, you will adopt a focused and disciplined approach. Make it clear that there is a time and place for socialising, but during training, your primary focus is on learning and progressing.

Lead by Example: Demonstrate your dedication through consistent effort, discipline, and progress. Your dedication may inspire your friend to take training more seriously. Be a positive role model in your training sessions.

Find Common Ground: Identify areas where you can both benefit from training together. Explore shared interests or goals that align with your training sessions, which can keep the friendship intact while still allowing for progress.

Seek Additional Training Partners: If your friend's approach consistently hinders your progress and causes frustration, consider seeking additional training partners or joining a class where you can surround yourself with individuals who share your level of commitment.

Maintain Perspective: Remember that martial arts is a personal journey, and each person progresses at their own pace. While your paths may diverge in training intensity, it doesn't have to negatively impact your friendship if you communicate openly and respect each other's choices.

Ultimately, the key is finding a balance that allows you to pursue your martial arts goals while maintaining a positive relationship with your friend. It may take time and effort, but with clear communication and mutual understanding, you can navigate this situation successfully.

Best of luck.

image: Djordje Stojiljkovic

Help! children are ruining my training sessions. I am in the beginner's class at my karate class and there are quite a few children in the class. They always muck up and slow the pace of the class. I understand we are a small club, but how can I encourage them to behave without looking like an 'asshole'? I need my training time too.

Dear Martial Artist,
It's understandable that you want to make the most of your training sessions, but it's important to approach this situation with empathy and consideration for the children and their parents. Here are some steps you can take to address the issue without coming across as harsh:

Talk to the Instructor: Start by discussing your concerns with your karate instructor privately. Share your perspective on how the children's behavior is affecting your training experience. In many cases, instructors are already aware of such issues and can make adjustments or provide guidance.

Offer to Assist: If you feel comfortable and have the skills to do so, offer to assist the instructor during certain parts of the class. This could involve helping the younger students with their techniques, keeping them engaged, or even demonstrating proper behavior and focus.

Talk to the Parents: If appropriate, have a respectful conversation with the parents of the children involved. Express your concern in a non-confrontational manner, focusing on how their children's behavior affects the overall quality of the class for everyone.

Suggest Separate Classes: If your club has enough members, you could suggest the idea of having separate classes for adults and children, especially if the age and skill gap is significant. This would allow both groups to train at their own pace without hindering each other's progress.

Lead by Example: During training, set a positive example by demonstrating focus, discipline, and respect for the instructor and fellow students. Your dedication can inspire others, including the children, to follow suit.

Supportive Encouragement: When you notice a child making an effort or behaving well, offer words of encouragement and praise. This can reinforce positive behavior and create a more cooperative atmosphere.

Patience and Understanding: Remember that children are still learning and may not fully grasp the expectations of a karate class. Try to exercise patience and understanding, recognizing that they too are there to learn and grow.

Seek Alternatives: If you find that the situation doesn't improve and it significantly impacts your training, consider discussing alternative training options with your instructor, such as private lessons or advanced classes.

Approaching the issue with empathy, open communication, and a willingness to collaborate with both the instructor and parents can help create a more harmonious training environment for everyone involved.

Send your dojo questions to the Doctor at: info@martialartsmagazineaustralia.com
please note that the Dojo Dr isn't technically a Doctor, they are more of a consultant, a sage even...

Yoga for the Martial Arts Body

by Maria Francis

I sincerely hope that stretching after warmup and following cool down is part of your training regime, but have you thought about taking it a step further? Have you asked yourself about the benefits of cross-training in another modality? Have you thought of trying Yoga? Regularly practised, Yoga can help improve flexibility, balance, strength, and mental focus, all of which are valuable attributes to a martial artist.

Warrior II (Virabhadrasana II):
Warrior II is excellent for building strength and stability in the legs, while also increasing hip flexibility and opening the chest.
Benefit: Strong legs are essential for powerful kicks and stances in karate. Improved hip flexibility can help with agility and ease of movement during sparring.

Tree Pose (Vrksasana):
Tree Pose is a balance pose that strengthens the muscles in the legs and core while improving concentration and focus.
Benefit: Enhanced balance and concentration are crucial in karate, especially for maintaining stable stances and reacting quickly to opponents.

Stand erect, keep your eyes focused. Shift your weight to one leg then lift the other and bring to rest on the inside of your standing leg. (avoiding the knee) lift your arms and bring your palms together over your head.

Downward Dog (Adho Mukha Svanasana)
Downward Dog is a full-body stretch that primarily targets the hamstrings, calves, and shoulders. It also helps improve balance and posture.
Benefit: Enhanced hamstring flexibility can improve kicking techniques and allow for higher, more controlled kicks. Better shoulder mobility can improve arm movements and blocking techniques.

Position yourself so that your front foot is at a right angle to your knee and calf. Your back thigh is parallel to the ground, back foot is on 45 degree angle. Lift up through torso, reach with fingertips, hold and breathe.

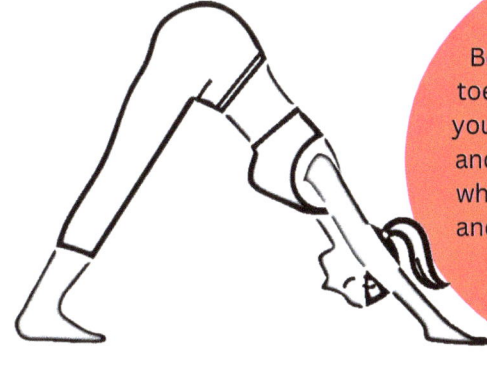

Begin in table top - tuck toes under and straighten your legs, push your palms and heels into the ground, while lifting your buttocks and keeping ears between your arms.

Cat-Cow Pose (Marjaryasana-Bitilasana):

This dynamic duo of poses helps to warm up and mobilize the spine. Cat Pose rounds the back, while Cow Pose arches it.

Benefit: A supple spine allows for better torso rotation, which is essential for generating power in punches and blocks. It also helps with overall body awareness and control.

> Kneel in table position. Knees under hips and arms beneath shoulders. Exhale- drop your head and tailbone, draw navel to your spine. Inhale raise your head and tailbone, curve your back and look to the ceiling. Repeat.

Pigeon Pose (Eka Pada Rajakapotasana):

Pigeon Pose is a hip-opening stretch that can relieve tension in the hips and lower back.

Benefit: Improved hip flexibility can enhance the range of motion for kicks and stances, making it easier to execute techniques with precision and power.

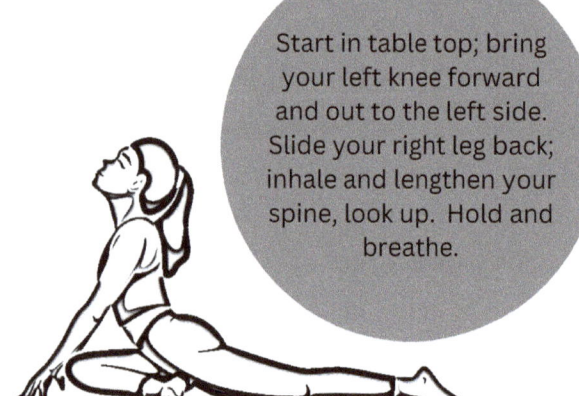

> Start in table top; bring your left knee forward and out to the left side. Slide your right leg back; inhale and lengthen your spine, look up. Hold and breathe.

Maria is a Certified Yoga Teacher - she teaches by appointment only. Currently her schedule is full but thankfully, she is working on her first book - Yoga for the Martial Arts Body.

images by Dimpleo-o

Cobra Pose (Bhujangasana):

Cobra Pose helps strengthen the muscles of the back, particularly the lower back, and opens up the chest, stretching the front of the body.

Benefit: A strong lower back can assist in maintaining an upright posture during karate stances and improve back support during bending movements. Chest opening can improve lung capacity for better endurance

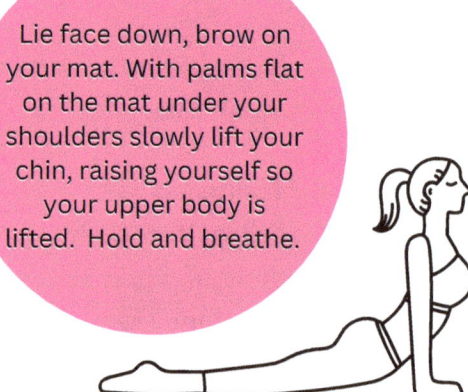

> Lie face down, brow on your mat. With palms flat on the mat under your shoulders slowly lift your chin, raising yourself so your upper body is lifted. Hold and breathe.

Plank Pose (Phalakasana):

Plank Pose is an isometric strength exercise that targets the core, shoulders, and upper back.

Benefit: A strong core is crucial for maintaining balance and stability during karate movements and can help generate power in strikes and blocks. Strong shoulders aid in punching and blocking techniques.

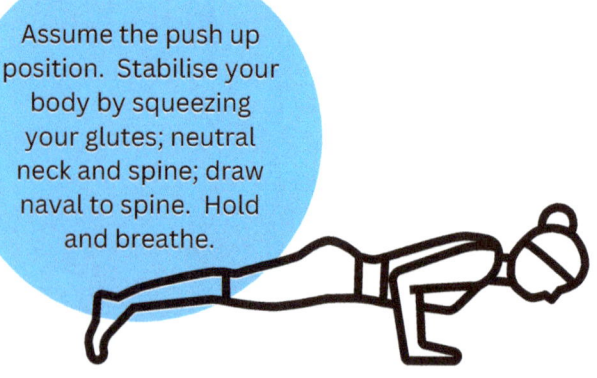

> Assume the push up position. Stabilise your body by squeezing your glutes; neutral neck and spine; draw naval to spine. Hold and breathe.

New Beginnings with Aikido
by Duncan Mitchell

I had a stroke in July 2016, which left me, completely paralysed down my left side and with a left side vision loss. After years of playing competitive sport, I was now a paraplegic.

I had played squash to a decent level and golf to a 12 handicap. I suddenly found myself unable to play any sports but I could walk and my arm movement was coming back, so I needed something to drive me and focus on. I'd always wanted to try a martial art, but I never had the time with three kids, work and other pursuits, until I found myself divorced, unemployed, living on my own.

I saw an advert to come and try Aikido, I was aware of Aikido through movies, etc. but didn't know anyone who practiced it. I had friends who did BJJ, kickboxing and taekwondo. My eldest son, who was 21 was starting boxing, but I didn't really think I was capable of these. I went along to West Coast Aikido in Wangara to chat with Sensei Ross Taylor to explain my health issues and see if I could try. I received a very warm welcome and once on the mats I found I could get along quite well. The instructors were aware of my limitations and cut me some slack while still making sure I put in the effort to the best of my abilities. I still have some left knee issues, so I have some problems rolling, but apart from that, I can manage most techniques pretty well.

I found the grading system and curriculum gave me a structure and progression which motivated me and getting my first tip on my white belt was a big milestone which spurred me on.

I've been training twice a week for a couple of years now and recently graduated to yellow belt, still a beginner, but my confidence has grown so much.

From being in a wheelchair to where I am now has been a long and tough road and Aikido has played a big part in that, not only from a physical aspect but the physiology and principles have played an important role in my mental health. The help and mentoring I've received from all the senior belts and instructors has been amazing. Although Aikido is often judged harshly by some, I think the fundamental principles and techniques are very powerful and I love it. I think more people should try it.

Top Tips
- Give it a try, you'll never know how capable you are until you try.
- Talk to the instructors about any injuries or limitations you have.
- Find a Dojo you like, ask about a trial membership.
- When you commit to a training/attendance program stick to it.
- Try the techniques and modify to what works for you, a slightly modified technique can still have the same outcome.
- Work within your limits, the more you do the wider your limits will become.
- Practice at home, there is lots of content online these days.
- Study techniques of senior belts, don't be afraid to ask, the only stupid question is the one not asked.
- When you are confident enough, share your knowledge with lower ranked belts.

Shihan Keiji Tomiyama

Shihan Tomiyama, returned to Western Australia in April 2023, to teach seminars throughout Kofukan Australia's metropolitan dojos for the first time since the pandemic.

Shihan Tomiyama is Joint Chief instructor of Kofukan international together with Naoki Omi, who is based in France. Shihan Tomiyama is also the Chief Instructor of Kofukan England and in 2022 he was awarded the rank of 9th Dan by the English Karate Federation and declared a living legend amongst karateka.

While in WA, Sensei Brian Chambers sat down to chat with Shihan Tomiyama.

Brian Chambers: What have you enjoyed about karate?

Shihan Tomiyama: My main purpose for Karate is to become better, to get to a higher level. The pursuit of getting to a higher level is my number one pleasure. Meeting people, our members are nice people, spending time together – training, eating, talking. That is my pleasure, yes.

Brian Chambers: We changed from Tani-ha Shito-ryu to Kofukan Shito-ryu. How did that eventuate and what is the difference between the two?

Shihan Tomiyama: Technically, there is no change at all. We have been Kofukan all the time with myself and Shihan Omi as leaders since 1981. (Shihan Yasuhiro Suzuki was the leader before that.) Both of us are students of Master Chojiro Tani, founder of Tani-ha Shito-ryu, so was Sensei Okubo. So the Kofukan organization was affiliated with the Tani-ha Shito-ryu Shukokai organization naturally. When Master Tani died, we naturally remained within Tani-ha Shito-ryu Shukokai with Master Tani's son Hiroshi Tani as the new leader (Soke).

As time went by, it became apparent that the new Soke and we have different ideas. So, in 2017, considering that we had been supporting the new Soke for 20 years and in doing so had repaid our debt of 30 years being students to his father, we decided to withdraw from the Tani-ha Shito-ryu Shukokai organization.

Brian Chambers: This is the 50th year anniversary 2022, year of the tiger. How has that been celebrated throughout the organisation?

Shihan Tomiyama: Shihan Omi and I came to Europe in 1972 and our most senior members have been supporting us since around that time. So, in 2022, we awarded them with new Dan grades and titles. But as we were in lock down due to Covid, we were unable to physically do anything to celebrate. Everything started moving again from this year.

Brian Chambers: How has the Kofukan organisation progressed or grown over the last fifteen years?

Shihan Tomiyama: I decided to promote our Karate outside our existing countries in 1991 because I thought our Karate was unique and different from many other schools and I had better let the world see what we were doing. So I started travelling to new parts of the world. We had just eight member countries in Europe then. I travelled to Oceania, India, Middle East, Southern Africa, North and South America and Eastern Europe. After some years, Kofukan had spread to more than 25 countries.

For the last ten to fifteen years, I did not try to expand the organization because I wanted both to achieve a higher level myself and to help our members to get to a higher level. I wanted to improve the quality inside the Association. I considered that our expansion period was probably over and that I might not have enough time to teach our Karate to a sufficient level in new countries, especially now as I get older.

Brian Chambers: Looking back on your career – what are your greatest moments, most memorable moments, and what would you have done differently?

Shihan Tomiyama: The most memorable moment of my Karate life was when I trained with Master Fujimoto for the first time. I always wanted to become better but, when I became an International Referee and travelled round Europe with the English National Team, I realized that Sport Karate was not what I was looking for. When I visited my university karate club in 1980, I met Masters Yamashita and Uehara, also graduates of the university. They were teaching what they had learnt from Master Kenwa Mabuni, founder of Shito-ryu. I thought it was probably the Karate I was looking for.

I went back to Japan in 1982 and stayed there for three years due to my father's illness. At that time, Master Yamashita persuaded Master Fujimoto, who had been refusing to teach, to start teaching. At the first training session with Master Fujimoto, I was totally convinced that it was the Karate I had been looking for.

We only live once, and I found what I was looking for. I feel very lucky.

Brian Chambers: In the past you have been doing some seminars with Wado ryu instructors in the UK. What is your relationship with the Wado-ryu clubs, and do you have a ranking with Wado-ryu?

Shihan Tomiyama: Sensei Shiomitsu, a Wado-ryu instructor, proposed to all Japanese instructors who were resident in the UK (except seniors like Masters Enoeda and Tatsuo Suzuki) and Ireland to get together and exchange ideas to better ourselves in the 1980s. Initially, one Shotokan, one Shito (myself) and five Wado instructors got together and held one training course. Since then, we had two training sessions as well as one course per year. After the first course, the Shotokan instructor pulled out of the group so it became a Wado and Shito course. A Wado instructor teaches Wado and I teach Shito. I do not practise the Wado style and do not have any ranking with Wado.

Brian Chambers: I have seen the applications of your karate to be like building blocks that form levels, with each level adding to become more complex fighting levels or systems. We have seen you do Uechi style kata is the way that you perform these kata a planned progression of your Shito-ryu style - another level of your fighting system as opposed to just performing another Uechi-ryu kata or a kata from another style. Have you put your personal style and applications into this Uechi kata or is this the original kata from those that taught it?

Shihan Tomiyama: These Katas are what I learned from Master Fujimoto. As I mentioned earlier, these are the Karate I was looking for. I learnt Doshisha Goju-ryu (Naha-te from Master Kenwa Mabuni) from Masters Yamashita and Uehara and these Katas (Master Fujimoto named his style En-ryu) are the backbone of my Karate. Katas we practise within Kofukan are Tani-ha Shito-ryu Katas. I learnt from Master Tani but technical and fighting principles are from Masters Fujimoto, Yamashita and Uehara.

If my Karate is different from other Shito-ryu people, this is the reason. Also, if you see Uechi Katas performed by mainstream Uechi people, they are different from how I do them.

Master Fujimoto learnt these Katas from Master Seijiro Sakihama, founder of Jugo-Shizen-ryu, who had learnt from Master Kanbun Uechi, founder of Uechi-ryu.

Brian Chambers: The technical principal of using the whole body in many of your applications, including Kobudo, is there some similarities with the Japanese arts of kendo and sumo with the way you use whole body in karate?

Shihan Tomiyama: Like Karate, there are two kinds of Kendo, modern (sports) Kendo and old (traditional) Kendo (Kenjutsu). Old Kendo has lots of similarity to my Karate using the old Martial Arts principles of Japan. Master Fujimoto practiced Kendo from a young age before starting Karate. He used principles of Miyamoto Musashi to explain his Karate.

Jodo, which I have practised for the last 30 years or so, is one of the traditional Japanese Martial Arts and I have learnt quite a lot from it. I do not think Sumo has much in common with Karate, although I enjoy watching it.

Brian Chambers: During the COVID outbreak how did you use your time – traditional karate practise, study, developing drills, trumpet practise?

Shihan Tomiyama: I slept more, started watching YouTube, wrote Kata booklets etc. Karate wise, it was not much different although I did not teach. And, yes, I played trumpet.

Brian Chambers: Can we expect to see you publish any more books or education videos?

Shihan Tomiyama: Maybe. Hopefully, something new can be produced.

Brian Chambers: The pin'an bunkai kumite you developed is lethal. Can we expect to see more of this kind of drills for other katas?

Shihan Tomiyama: Again, maybe. Those senior people who train with me regularly have learnt my ideas.

Brian Chambers: Have you thought about designing your own kata?

Shihan Tomiyama: No. There are already enough Katas.

Brian Chambers: There is a photo of you and sensei Omi with no gi jacket and big muscles – how did you get those muscles?

Shihan Tomiyama: At university, we trained very hard. Training lasted three hours. Roughly speaking, one-hour physical training, one hour basics and one hour fighting. Every day, we did a minimum of 500 sit-ups. At training camps, we had three sessions a day, and we did 1000 sit-ups in each session. Once, we did 2500 sit-ups continuously. We did a lot of physical training. At that time, there was no control in chudan punches and kicks, so we had to be strong. Shihan Omi and I continued in the same way during our early days in Europe and our senior members remember that well.

Brian Chambers: What other exercises did you used to do during training?

Shihan Tomiyama: Exercises were fairly simple. Press-ups, sit-ups and squats. Only the numbers were big, several hundreds to a thousand. Also, we did lots of basics. A thousand punches, hundreds of kicks, basic stances up and down the dojo many times. Once in a training camp, we did two hours of Shiko-dachi, non-stop. Hard training develops will power.

Brian Chambers: Is there any legacy or message to the world about your karate that you are leaving behind?

Shihan Tomiyama: Originally, I had an idea (or desire) to make several books to cover all Tani-ha Shito-ryu Katas. But, making books is a very big task and I do not think I will manage to complete the task. So, I wrote a description of all Tani-ha Shito-ryu Katas in English and distributed those to our senior people in five PDF booklets.

The orders of Katas are one thing, but I hope our higher graded people have learnt my principles of Karate which I have accumulated over the years.

Brian Chambers: Have you considered writing an autobiography?
Shihan Tomiyama: No.

Brian Chambers: What would be your advice to people that are practicing karate or want to practise karate to become successful in performing karate?
Shihan Tomiyama: Learn and practise proper basics and basic katas which teach our principles. Once you understand the principles, it is much easier to develop yourself.

Brian Chambers: The change over from Tani-ha to Kofukan Shito-ryu the announcement was at the eightieth anniversary of Doshisha University. Your relationship with karate is essential through Doshisha University, and you haven't been to Doshisha training since covid.

Shihan Tomiyama: Doshisha University Karate Club is the home of our Karate. It was established in 1937 with Chojun Miyagi, founder of Goju-ryu, as its Technical Director. Then it was handed over to Kenwa Mabuni, founder of Shito-ryu. Masters Tani, Fujimoto, Yamashita and Uehara are all graduates of the club. So are Shihan Omi and I.

Covid stopped everything all over the world. But I have been to Doshisha this year. So things are getting back to normal gradually.

Books by Shihan Tomiyama

Available where all good books are sold!

For more information about Kofukan Karate Australia and upcoming seminars with Shihan Tomiyama
https://kofukankarateaustralia.com/

International events
https://www.kofukankarate.com

Sensei Brian Chambers runs Kofukan Karate Kalgoorlie and he can be contacted at:
kofukankalgoorlie@gmail.com

Early Shukokai Training Part II
by Sensei Don Godwin

Sensei Kimura's first course was like an earthquake in the club. In a good way! Sensei Kimura had trained with Sensei Tani and was encouraged under his leadership to explore the science of hitting. I'm sure in every Shukokai dojo, you will find impact pads. Sensei Kimura wanted something that felt like hitting a body and found it in a high-density foam. The pads protect the holder from the true force generated by the technique, but give an indication of what it would feel like to be hit without the pad. Good impact is felt in a small but deeper area than the accompanying "push", which shoves the person back. To put in another way, pure impact would punch out a fist size hole in a sheet of paper, while leaving the rest of the sheet intact and unmoved.

We embraced the new way of punching and copied it to other techniques. The grading had seen some promotions, Sandy, Graham and everyone else had gone up a level. Mokesh, my Indian mentor, was now a green belt. A few guys, including some seniors from school, had joined. We had a new white belt in Piet Serfontein. He was super dedicated, and an excellent technician, always training before class, while the rest of us chatted.

In due course, Sensei Kimura returned. We had another influx of South African black belts. Among them was a very attractive blond lady, the first female karateka I had ever seen. She was not treated any differently with one exception.

Sensei Kimura had worked on Sanchin kata and told us to remove our gi jackets to show the muscle and breathing movement fundamental to the kata. As she began to remove her belt, Sensei quickly said, No! not you – with a chuckle. If I'm not mistaken, Sensei Kimura moved the goal posts again. We had adapted to the double hip twist, but he now eliminated one half of the technique. Looking back over years of training with Sensei, he was always tinkering, always moving forward towards his ultimate objective – perfect impact. For us mortals, it was not easy to adapt, and for someone like me, who was happy with continuity, highly challenging.

So, from the double hip twist (and the occasional accidental triple twist), we had to relearn a different way. Of course, there was no going back. If I guess correctly, Sensei had assessed that taking the hip back was adding time and the technique would work faster if the torque was there in the first place. He eliminated the initial movement by having the hip forward, and the elbow fully pulled back before release. This created the necessary torque as the chest muscles acted against the hip with an effect like a stretched rubber band.

Another grading loomed, but I was more confident this time and passed. There had been a change in the grading system. We now went White, Yellow, Orange, Green, Blue & three grades of Brown. I graded to Orange. Some of the black belts who had come to Sensei Kimura's course had joined permanently. They were most likely local from other styles, but some of the South Africans may well have stayed. I was astounded to see quiet Piet Serfontein, wearing a black belt. I thought at the time that his dedication had paid off, but more probably he was a black belt in another style and had chosen to don a white belt until he had been assessed. He remained humble; once watching him practice before class, and secretly admiring his ability, he remarked, "I think I'm just getting the hang of oizuki". The same could not be said of some of the new black belts.

Don Godwin (5th Dan Shukokai) instructs in Karrinyup. He has been training with Shukokai for over 50 years and teaching for 40. Shukokai is a fast, practical style and female friendly.
Contact Don on 0450 772 846 to arrange 2 weeks free training.

Sandy had emigrated and Graham was now the senior student, but one of the new ones, Brian, appointed himself the discipline enforcer, once hitting my friend Rob with a mawashi for talking in line. We learnt to keep quiet when Sensei Des was talking!
That was the last time I would train with Sensei Kimura for some years.

I would have been a blue belt when Enter the Dragon, starring Bruce Lee, hit the screens. Sensei Des got a group booking, and we all went along, keen to see this master. I did not know that Bruce Lee practiced Kung Fu and that no doubt influenced me and the others, but we were unimpressed. "Rubbish" was the consensus. No matter what we thought, he was to have a major impact on the martial arts world.

Master Kimura

Three Afghanistan war veterans set out on a motorcycle ride and run into an awkward situation which leads to them being chased by bikers, gangsters, and detectives.

This all ends with a standoff on a hill with instructions from Sarg played by Rod Power to instruct the other two Eddie and Shane to outflank them but to, "be careful not to hurt them too much."

The film stars: Edward Hope Black Belt Chinese Kickboxing Mixed Martial Arts; Shane Vuletich Muay Thai Instructor Former State Champion; Jeremy Allan 7th Dan Black belt Chinese Kickboxing Mixed Martial Arts 2 times Gold Medalist Arafura Games BOXING Oceania Silver Bronze Medalists .. 2 Time Australian OPEN Martial Ats Champion.

The film will be finished by the end of 2023, it will premiere at ACE cinema in Midland, and it will be simultaneously launched in International Film Festivals.

Starring Edward Hope Black Belt Chinese Kickboxing Mixed Martial Arts
Shane Vuletich Muay Thai Instructor Former State Champion
Jeremy Allan 7th Dan Black belt Chinese Kickboxing Mixed Martial Arts 2 times Gold Medalist Arafura Games BOXING Oceania Silver Bronze Medalists .. 2 Time Australian OPEN Martial Ats Champion
The movie has many fighters from Sports Combat Nathan Clarke (The Dreaded One) Trained by Shane Vuletich.
The film will be finished by the end of the year 2023

Rod Power 10th Dan Master of Martial Arts with 48 years teaching experience.
6 Times Australian Open Martial Arts Champion; 2 Times Australasian Open Martial Arts Champion; 15 Times State Open Champion.

Seventy Lashes

The Seventy Lashes of Wisdom

by Al Ghoniem

As I stood before the assembled audience, bare-chested and clad only in shorts, the conclusion ceremony commenced, and I braced myself for the symbolic seventy lashes. Each strike would mark the end of my profound journey through the art of Lian Padukan, an odyssey of self-discovery, transformation, and enlightenment that had sculpted the very essence of my being.

The first lash descended upon my arms like a thunderous strike of fate, awakening memories of my tumultuous childhood. Born with a rare genetic condition, I endured the relentless taunts of bullies and the cruel clutches of prejudice. Seeking solace, I turned to the ancient fighting arts, a sanctuary that transmuted the feeble child within me into a tempestuous force of unyielding strength.

With the second lash upon my head, the echoes of my revered masters, PakTuan Ayahanda, Haji Hashim, Bin Salleh, and Cikgo Ayahanda Haji Azhar, reverberated through the corridors of my soul. They bestowed upon me a revelation that transcended the bounds of mere combat—a truth that unveiled the power of the mind, an arsenal of infinite possibilities to decipher the enigmas of existence. Lian Padukan metamorphosed into a manifestation of profound philosophy, guiding me to confront life's battles with a warrior's spirit and a philosopher's discernment.

The lashes upon my chest evoked the image of a valorous warrior, standing resolute against the tempestuous gales of adversity. From overcoming physical limitations to ascending the towering peaks of software engineering, the crucible of life had forged an indomitable spirit—a spirit of audacity that dared to dream beyond the limitations of convention.

With an unexpected lash upon my groin, desire and discipline engaged in a fierce ballet of inner turmoil. The wiles of temptations sought to ensnare my soul, yet I stood unwavering, an embodiment of virtue and self-restraint. The trials of relationships and the deceitful dance with love left their marks upon my heart, but I emerged not broken, but fortified, my resolve unshakable, my spirit unyielding.

The lashes upon my back brought forth the haunting spectre of betrayal, akin to the malevolent Kuntilanak of folklore.

The sinister blades of deceit pierced my trust, leaving scars of treachery upon my soul. Yet, from the shards of shattered trust emerged a revelation, in the grace of Allah's infinite mercy I received a twofold compensation of love and care, as if the heavens themselves blessed me with righteous, sincere, and loving souls to accompany my profound journey. Their presence became pillars of strength and solace, guiding me through trials with unwavering support. Their love, a gentle breeze from the heavens, whispered comfort to my heart and uplifted my spirit. In their care, I found a sanctuary of peace where worldly burdens dissipated.

The lashes upon my legs symbolized the ceaseless pilgrimage of knowledge and wisdom. Like a nomadic seeker traversing the deserts of eternity, I journeyed far from my origins, immersing myself in diverse cultures and ancient wisdom. This odyssey had transformed me into an intrepid explorer, a seeker of truth that traversed the horizons of knowledge without fear or falter.

With each step away from the testing ground, I carried within me the indomitable spirit of a Muslim warrior—a spirit of resilience that had transcended flesh and blood, a spirit that mirrored the enigmatic dance of the universe. The journey of seventy lashes had etched an indelible tapestry upon my soul—a tapestry interwoven with the threads of profound philosophy, unwavering courage, enduring love, and the insatiable quest for knowledge.

As I ventured forth into the vast horizon of existence, my heart swelled with gratitude and determination. For this ceremony had marked not just an end, but a beginning—a dawning of the next chapter in the boundless odyssey of life and martial arts. And so, with a heart ablaze with passion, purpose, and wisdom, I embraced whatever destiny Allah had inscribed for me, knowing that I had become a living testament to the deeper artistry of Lian Padukan—a masterpiece of the human spirit itself.

In the vast and diverse landscape of martial arts, one discipline that stands out for its unique blend of physical prowess and spiritual growth is Lian Padukan. Rooted in the rich cultural heritage of Southeast Asia, Lian Padukan is a martial art that goes beyond mere combat techniques; it encompasses a philosophy of harmony, discipline, and self-improvement.

Originating in Indonesia, where it was developed as a synthesis of various traditional martial arts systems. The name "Lian Padukan" itself is derived from Indonesian and signifies "the path to unity." This name perfectly encapsulates the core principles of this martial art, which emphasises the unity of mind, body, and spirit.

At the heart of Lian Padukan lies a deep philosophical foundation that seeks to promote harmony, both within oneself and with the surrounding world. Practitioners are encouraged to cultivate virtues such as respect, humility, and self-control. It teaches not only how to defend oneself physically but also how to maintain emotional balance and mental clarity in the face of adversity.

Lian Padukan incorporates a wide range of techniques, including striking, grappling, and self-defence manoeuvres. What sets it apart is the emphasis on fluidity and adaptability in combat. Practitioners are encouraged to adapt their techniques to the situation at hand, making Lian Padukan effective in various scenarios. (ed)

The Place of Traditional Karate-do in the Modern Martial Arts Landscape

by Grant Brechney

For many decades, the traditional practice of Karate-do was coveted by martial arts enthusiasts of all types since the Japanese masters began introducing their mystical art to the rest of the world. Foreigners engaged in training and immersed themselves not only in the physical aspect of the practice, but mental, spiritual, and cultural components as well. With the rise in popularity of mixed martial arts (MMA), however, the western attitude toward martial arts has undergone a palpable shift away from many of the traditional underpinnings of systems such as Karate-do, in favour of focusing on the practicality and technical efficacy associated with success in one-on-one unarmed combat. As a result of this cultural shift, the traditional martial arts have come under intense scrutiny regarding their effectiveness, traditions, and overall place within this new modern landscape of martial arts cross-training. In this writer's opinion, this is both a good and a bad thing, however, those who wish for the traditional martial arts to survive into this new era must understand, and be able to articulate, what valuable benefits come specifically from training in more traditional martial arts, and why these are important for those interested merely in becoming the modern combat athlete.

Culture in general is subject to constant development which can often start with a single person's eccentric idea, that persistently espoused over time, can become a newly accepted norm. The culture of martial arts training is no different. Many factors have had a significant influence on the way the martial arts industry operates in the modern day, and more pertinently, on how the general population perceives the martial arts, both traditional and modern. Distinct among these, are the development of technology and social media, and a competitive martial arts promotion called the Ultimate Fighting Championship (UFC). Both key elements have irrevocably changed the landscape of martial arts forever. Without going into too much historical backdrop in this article, the primary cultural shift, popularly propagated by the UFC, was the undeniable truth that in one-on-one unarmed combat, an athlete can achieve the most success if trained in a variety of martial arts skills that included effective striking, ground fighting, and transitionary fighting (transitions from a standing position to the ground or vice versa). Due to the extensive range of skills required, and the relative shortness of time in which combat athletes need to develop high levels of proficiency in these skills, any aspect of more traditional training that does not directly contribute to the goal of being the best combat athlete one can possibly be, is deemed as irrelevant material that can simply be discarded from training. The question we, as traditional martial arts practitioners, should ask ourselves is, is this approach incorrect? If so, why?

My answer to this question is a little more complex than a simple yes or no. There have undoubtedly been good and bad effects of this new philosophy of training in comparison to more traditional methods. These are important to articulate if we wish to ensure the longevity of systems such as Karate-do into the future. Furthermore, examination of this topic requires those that engage with it do so with an unbiased and rational mind. Think, for a moment, back to the days of when you first started your own journey in martial arts. You would have undoubtedly approached some kind of instructor with a high degree of proficiency and dedicated yourself to their teachings with one or more goals in mind that you wanted to achieve. What were those goals? I'd be willing to bet my last dollar that one of them was to become more effective in defending yourself in unsolicited combat. Why else would you start training martial arts? If someone simply sought to get fitter, make new friends, try to learn any kind of new skill, they could do any other physical activity which would achieve all those things. What distinguishes those that seek out martial arts, is a desire to improve their ability to defend themselves if required. This is a very admirable goal and one that I always challenge every single student that walks through my door, to hold forever in their minds.

Combat sports have heavily influenced the context of training in many dojos and training centres. The rules of these various combat sports change the nature of the techniques practiced daily, and this becomes more pronounced as the focus of the dojo is driven further toward competition rather than equipping their students with the most effective defensive and offensive skills in martial arts. Karate is a prime example of this. There can be no doubt that sport Karate training is very effective in developing a sport Karate athlete, however, the skills and techniques needed to be successful in this competition format do not effectively translate to a real combat situation, and the rules of sport Karate competition are the reason for this. Strikes are only permitted to certain areas of the body, protective equipment is worn, a certain level of contact in strikes is unacceptable and punished for example. Put simply, we are what we train habitually. Let's look at MMA competition by comparison now. This competition format has far less rules than sport Karate. Athletes are encouraged to damage their opponents far more than would ever be acceptable in sport Karate competition. Therefore, the training and techniques developed translate far better in terms of their efficacy and effectiveness to a situation where one needs to defend themselves against an assailant. On the other hand, there have been many athletes that have competed in the UFC that come from Karate backgrounds such as Michelle Waterson, Bas Ruten, George Siant Pierre, one from even my own style of Shorinjiryu Karate-do, Alexandra Chambers. We can deduce from this, that there is still a place for effective Karate training in the highest levels of one-on-one unarmed combat then. All that's required, is training methodologies of the style within a less restrictive competitive context. After all, Karate was initially developed as a martial arts system specifically designed to defend oneself as effectively as possible.

and offensive skills in martial arts. Karate is a prime example of this. There can be no doubt that sport Karate training is very effective in developing a sport Karate athlete, however, the skills and techniques needed to be successful in this competition format do not effectively translate to a real combat situation, and the rules of sport Karate competition are the reason for this. Strikes are only permitted to certain areas of the body, protective equipment is worn, a certain level of contact in strikes is unacceptable and punished for example. Put simply, we are what we train habitually. Let's look at MMA competition by comparison now. This competition format has far less rules than sport Karate. Athletes are encouraged to damage their opponents far more than would ever be acceptable in sport Karate competition. Therefore, the training and techniques developed translate far better in terms of their efficacy and effectiveness to a situation where one needs to defend themselves against an assailant. On the other hand, there have been many athletes that have competed in the UFC that come from Karate backgrounds such as Michelle Waterson, Bas Ruten, George Siant Pierre, one from even my own style of Shorinjiryu Karate-do, Alexandra Chambers. We can deduce from this, that there is still a place for effective Karate training in the highest levels of one-on-one unarmed combat then. All that's required, is training methodologies of the style within a less restrictive competitive context. After all, Karate was initially developed as a martial arts system specifically designed to defend oneself as effectively as possible.

Karate-do however, is not solely focused on developing the most effective combat athlete. There are many other aspects of Karate-do training that permeate many different areas of one's life. Indeed, the suffix "do" at the end of the word Karate-do, refers in Japanese to "a way." In Japanese culture, being a practitioner of "a way" means that this practice involves a well thought-out and meaningful philosophy that is also included in the teachings and honoured by the students. Typically, this is practiced through detailed rituals that intersect almost every aspect of Karate-do training. These rituals are often layered with meaning and teachings that can often become far more important to the more experienced martial artist than pure proficiency in combat training. After all, one can only remain an athlete for so long. Eventually time will change the focus of your training, and although one should always strive for technical perfection in the combative aspect of training for as long as they continue, a deeper and more meaningful goal can take forefront of the mind of the more seasoned practitioner of the traditional art. Indeed, practicing the "way" of martial arts is far more profound than merely using them as vehicle for honing one's combative abilities. Thus, that is what we stand to lose should our martial arts traditions be lost to the sands of time, and such a loss would be a devastating blow.

About Grant Brechney:

Grant Brechney has studied in a variety of martial arts disciplines over more than two decades with a prolific competition history. He holds gradings in Shorinjiryu Karate-do (3rd Dan), Arjuken Karate/MMA (2nd Dan), Brazilian Jiu Jitsu (Brown Belt), Modern Arnis of the Philippines (Brown Belt) and regularly practices, Muay Thai, boxing, and wrestling.

Grant competed in hundreds of full-contact Karate competitions winning two world championships in Koshiki Karate at heavyweight and competed internationally on several occasions in Australia, Malaysia, and Canada. He won two amateur MMA titles and competed at the professional level in MMA in Australia. He won a Brazilian Jiu Jitsu world championship as a blue belt and has competed in over one-hundred other Brazilian Jiu Jitsu bouts.

Grant is a PhD candidate in his 5th year at Charles Sturt University in NSW. He is a published Exercise Scientist with a research focus on investigating the performance effects of weight cutting on combat sport athletes. He is the owner and head instructor of Karate, Brazilian Jitsu, and MMA at Ascend Martial Arts in Tweed Heads, NSW.

Instagram
https://www.instagram.com/thestorm.mma/
Facebook
https://www.facebook.co/TheStormMMA
Email - thestormma@gmail.com
Website – www.ascendmartialarts.com.au

Image Ryan McVay

How Karate Saved My Life

by Andy Kent

Did you ever wake up with no memory of the night before? I woke up three months later and I couldn't feel my legs. Can you imagine?

Staring at the hospital roof. I heard voices, but my body didn't work, I couldn't move to see who was talking or even understand what they were talking about. But I knew it wasn't good.

I didn't remember the accident. The day or weeks before. All I knew was the colour of the hospital roof.

What happened? What can I do now? How will I survive? Where am I?

I had travelled to Cambodia in 2009 to join the fight against human trafficking. One fateful night, I was in a motorcycle accident. Three months later I woke up, back in Australia. In hospital, surrounded by my family.

The doctor and nurses tip toed around me. I asked myself, how bad am I?

My family visits, eyes always full of tears, "Why are you crying, I am okay, I will be out soon."

It would have been easy to give up, and it crossed my mind many times, but I didn't. I took one day at a time, any every day I strived to be better than what I was yesterday. I was version two. Version one had been deleted from the game.

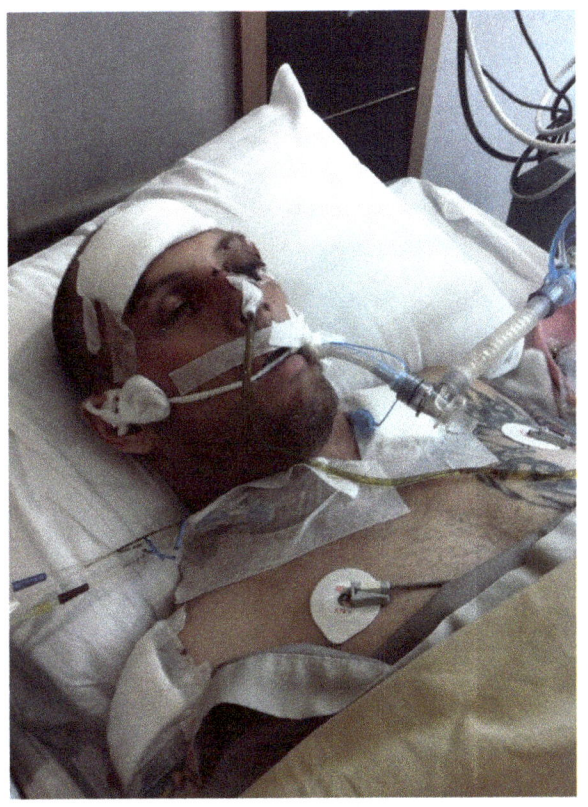

All my life I had been beaten down and beaten up. I learnt to stand through the greatest storms, avoid the greatest enemies. I spent many days at school standing in the naughty corner, learning to be comfortable alone with just my thoughts.

Karate taught me to accept the situation I was in and train hard to change the outcome of the next situation. Life is a continuous set of circumstances and your attitude will determine how you come through the other end.

STILL AIM FOR THE STARS, BUT DON'T RUN THERE.

In my mind, I would train my katas every day and dreamed of walking again. I set myself a goal to walk back into the hospital in Cambodia with the words, "Wheel me out and I will walk back!"

Karate taught me to train hard and change the outcome of the next situation. It would have been easier to give up, but I didn't.

I TRAIN AND TEACH KARATE EVERY DAY BECAUSE I HAVE FOUND THE MAGIC INSIDE KARATE, AND I HOPE TO SHARE IT WITH EVERYONE.

I started karate in 2001 under Go Kan Ryu in Australia, the largest Karate club in the World combining a mixture of Shotokan and Go-ju Karate. Winning several gold medals in kata and kumite in Australia I went on to compete in the 2007 G.K.R World Cup representing Australia.

In 2009, I moved to Cambodia and trained with Master Chea Nara, whilst also training with Shihan John Kirkham from ShimBuKai in Australia. In 2013 I was asked to open Shimbukai in South East Asia.

Contact: shimbukai.cambodia@gmail.com
Facebook: Shimbukai Karate Cambodia

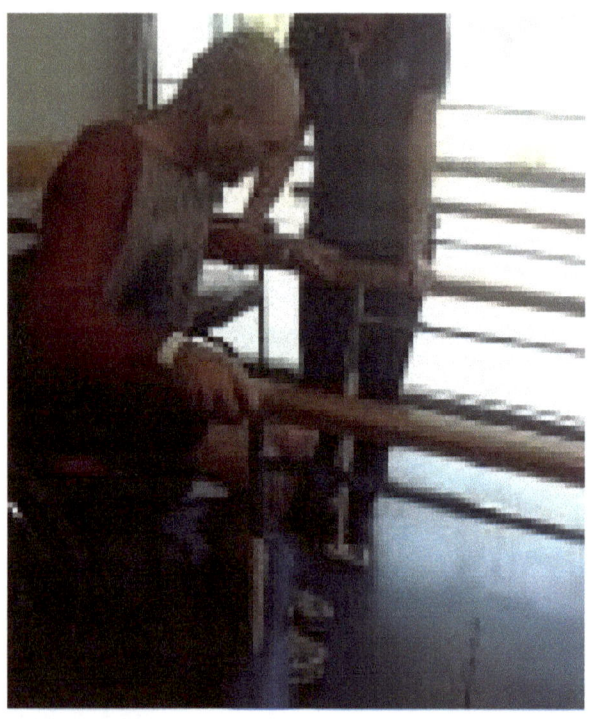

Watching the Tree

by Mike Clarke

In her book, Watching the Tree, author Adeline Yen Mah, passes on an anecdote told to her by her grandfather. At the time she was a thirteen-year-old girl living in Hong Kong and thinking of running away from home to live with an aunt in Shanghai. She had left the city with her mother at the age of ten and was convinced she could return and pick up her life there again, exactly where she'd left it three years earlier. Wondering if her grandfather would lend her the fare, she asked him, and explained what she intended to do once she got to Shanghai. The reply her grandfather gave was not the one she was hoping for. He did not loan her the money, but he gave her a gift that remained with her for the rest of her life. The gift was a story about experience and about change; it was a story about a boy, a hare, and a tree…

"Once, long ago in China, a young apprentice was told by his teacher to go into the forest and catch a hare for dinner: the young man took off full of excitement. However, as he had never hunted before he had no real idea how he was going to accomplish the task his teacher had set him. Shortly after entering the forest, he spotted a hare running very quickly along a path. Suddenly it turned and ran head on into a tree. Because it had been running so fast the impact with the tree killed it instantly, all the apprentice had to do was pick it up and bring it back to his teacher. The young man's triumph was short lived however, for even though he returned to the forest many times afterwards he was never able to bring back another hare. You see, whenever he went back to the forest, instead of looking for a hare to 'catch' he simply returned to the same tree, and there he sat, waiting for another hare to run in to it."

When I first read this story, it struck me that many karateka also spend their time, metaphorically speaking 'watching trees' instead of acquiring skill; and perhaps this is why so many karateka remain hungry for information. So hungry, in fact that they regularly attend seminars to train with instructors who, in many cases, have simply been 'watching a different tree' for a longer period of time. Had the young apprentice in the story learnt to catch a hare, even by trial-and-error, he would have developed a useful skill. He would have also come to understand that nothing in life (or hunting) stays the same. He would have discovered that each hunt would have to be conducted differently depending on the season and the conditions he found in the forest. He would have realised that there are fundamental rules he needed to follow, but the actual method he used could be adjusted to the prevailing conditions of the day.

The parallels with karate are clear, if as a karateka, you keep in mind that your first visit to a dojo is to 'study' karate, in time you will learn a useful skill. You will come to understand that no two training sessions are ever the same. You discover each session will see you face different challenges depending on the lesson. You will also come to realise that there are fundamental rules that need to be followed but the principles of karate will allow you to adjust your technique to suit your own body and the prevailing conditions of your health once you are skilled enough to understand karate's core principles. It is too bad that many karateka are not educated this way.

Many who are new to karate, and many who are not, are mistaken when it comes to where the 'fighting' is taking place;

erroneously believing that karate will help them defeat someone else; well, it might, but that's missing the point. In my book, Redemption, I traced the path to self-destruction my life was taking as an irascible teenage street fighter; and how, with a discipline first imposed by others, and later, by myself, karate training revealed a sense of purpose and the prospect of a life that up until then had evaded me. Hidden in plain sight but made visible only through the lens of sincere introspection, the 'way' of karate points directly to the source of human conflict: the mind. What goes on inside your mind determines, to a large extent, what happens in your world.

Beginners in karate are commonly pointed in the wrong direction, and because of that, quickly become attached to the things they first encounter, just as the apprentice became attached to the tree that killed the hare. Indeed, new karateka are often encouraged to cling to the very ideas and practises that will hinder their progress the most. For example, the focus on status, rank, and becoming a 'champion', diverts attention away from the real purpose of training in karate, which is to protect yourself (often from yourself). Becoming hooked on the external trappings of your training places you on a path leading you away from obtaining tenure of your karate, promoting instead, a sense of dependency on others.

When you 'watch the tree' in your mind, you fix yourself in a moment of time, ignoring the fact that time, like life, never stands still. You fail to appreciate that in order to grow as a human being you must learn to adapt to the changes time (and living) endlessly bring. Adaptations arise from failure, so you must learn to invest in that rather than hold your breath until you succeed in something. Many who walk away from karate once they have a 'black belt' and the rush of youth has ended, do so not for the reasons they provide to others, but because they have given up hope of another hare ever running in to the tree they have been doggedly watching for so long. Their failure to repeat the 'success' of their early years in karate becomes too much to deal with, and they simply give up the struggle. Few question if their failure to invest in their own shortcomings kept them looking for success in the wrong place.

Maybe, from time to time, if you have the courage, you should ask yourself... 'Am I a tree watcher?' Thinking about things like this is always helpful. Did you attach yourself early on to the wrong idea of what you were doing when you began training in karate? Did you, all be it unwittingly, step on to the dojo floor for the first time and on to a path that led you away from the very things you were searching for? When sitting in Mokuso, at the end of a hard training session maybe these are the kind of questions to be pondered. Focusing your effort solely on the physical techniques of karate that you enjoy or come easily to you is as much a tree watching exercise as filling your head with dreams of samurai, black belts, and becoming a karate 'master'.

Clearly, it is not possible to move forward while standing still. So, unless you are a believer in the maxim: all will come to those who sit and wait, it is important not to focus for too long on any one aspect of your (karate) education. Understanding karate is after all a 'feeling' for what you do, rather than merely the accumulation of information committed to memory. Watching a tree, regardless of the length of time you do it, won't bring you a single step closer to what you are looking for. How many karateka are learning something useful and how many are simply waiting for something to happen is a difficult question to answer. In my experience there are certainly more people training in karate than studying it, and far more 'instructors' masquerading as sensei than there are 'teachers'. When I consider how many karateka training today have learnt to 'catch a hare', and how many have simply sat and watched a tree, the future of authentic karate doesn't look good.

Thought and action, form and function, it's easy to see you need all four to make progress. If the concepts underpinning karate fail to become a normal part of who you are, then you are left with the alternative, the temporary ability to move your arms and legs in in ways that resemble karate. It is not enough to go to the dojo, and it is not enough to 'do' karate. If you want to grasp the value of it and to experience its physical and psychological benefits, you must enter the 'way' deeply.

Had the young apprentice in the story fully appreciated the good fortune of his situation the day his teacher sent him into the forest, it may well have taught him something of value; but he did not. He missed the point completely and spent the rest of his life desperately watching a tree.

About the Book

Author of bestselling 'Falling Leaves' weaves together for the same audience her own personal experiences with the best of Chinese philosophy. Adeline Yen Mah, whose autobiography 'Falling Leaves' is an international bestseller, here interweaves her own experiences with her views on Chinese thought and wisdom to create an illuminating and highly personal guide for Western readers.

POSSIBILITIES

Part 2
by
Daniel Fellow

Kaylee placed the broom against the hole-riddled wall and bent over to scoop up the scraps of paper and food wrappings that had been discarded in her dad's future dojo. In the week leading up to receiving the keys to the venue and a week after they had signed the lease, she had tried to make her Dad see reason. Kaylee had tried financial logic, she had pleaded, cajoled and argued with him. But always with the same effect. Her dad, Brian, had simply smiled and patted her cheek and gently said, "You'll see."

Now, resigned to helping her dad achieve his vision, she picked up the last of the rubbish and debris that had taken over a week and a half to sweep up and dispose of.

When she had first seen the inside of the shop, Kaylee had been appalled at the state and condition of the hall and the amount of rubbish littered throughout had been deceiving. A week and a half later, with the last rubbish bag filled to the brim, the hall was looking somewhat respectable.

Large and small gaping holes dotted the walls of the hall, left behind by angry and bored residents of the town. A hole in the floorboards, something she had started to call The Chasm, to her dad's amusement, was one of the hall's most dangerous features. In the first couple of days of the clean-up, she had nearly fallen in it half a dozen times, until she forced herself to walk to the immediate right upon entering the hall.

She couldn't wait until Monday when the carpenter was due to arrive and work his magic. *Or convince Dad that he's wasting his time and money,* she hoped silently.

Kaylee heard feet pounding on the footpath and she turned to see her father walk up to the threshold of the door, bow respectfully and then entered. In his hands was a rectangular box she had never seen before.

"What's that?" she asked, genuinely curious. She rose from her haunches and walked over to her dad, who opened the box with gentle ease and respect.

He glanced at her, his eyes twinkled mischievously and he winked. "The must-have furnishing every dojo needs."

A small list of items instantly ran through her mind as to what it could be. A pair of nunchaku? A belt holder? A stylised doormat that read "Wax On, Wax Off, Shoes Off"?

Brian opened the box and pulled out a small banner with six words printed in English and the corresponding Japanese translation directly next to each word. Kaylee knew what it was immediately.

"That's your first dojo addition?" She was mildly disappointed, yet not altogether surprised.

The small list of karate principles had been drilled into her from a very young age and, even though she couldn't speak or read Japanese, she knew what each one meant. "Karate starts and ends with these principles," Brian said, scanning the walls to find the most appropriate place to hang it. "Remember? That's what I taught you when you were young."

"How can I forget? You used to make me recite them while eating dinner. And I couldn't have dessert unless I said them all. And what they meant."

"You always had a good memory."

"Dad, I was six. I had a great memory."

"I don't think you ever missed out on dessert."

Brian chuckled to himself and spotted a small, rusty nail. He walked over to it and hung the small banner from a string on the back of the banner.

He stepped back from the banner and read from it. "Reigi, sonkei, nintai, doryoku, sozo, yuki."

Without being prompted by her Dad, Kaylee recited the English translation. The words she had said over and over again when she had been a little girl. "Etiquette, respect, perseverance, effort, creativity, courage."

Brian turned to his daughter, placed an arm over her shoulders and drew her in. "You've still got it," he said. "I think that earned you a chocolate sundae on the way home."

She playfully elbowed him in the ribs. "Make sure it's got a flake in it. I deserve that much after all this cleaning I've been doing."

"What do you mean?" he said, looking about the hall, a look of comical befuddlement on his face. "This place is clean as. What have you done exactly?"

She punched him in the arm and went to throw another when he jumped back and blocked it. He pretended to throw his own but she effortlessly avoided the playfully thrown jab. She couldn't count the times they had playfully sparred over the years. Her dad almost always let her win when she was younger. But when she became older the sparring matches took on a more important learning aspect which taught her important self-defence principles that aided her in earning her own black belt.

Suddenly and without any preamble, Brian dropped down into a stance and started to perform his favourite kata.

"Really, Dad? Bassai Dai?" After nearly an entire day of cleaning, the last thing she wanted to do was train in a dilapidated hall.

"Yep, really. Come on. Let's see if you've still got it."

Kaylee followed suit and she performed the kata alongside her Dad, like she had done many times in the past.

A small, nervous cough from the doorway forced them to stop and turn in that direction.

A boy of about thirteen or fourteen was standing outside the doorway eating an ice cream that was starting to melt.

"My friend Bobby said this was going to be a karate shop or something. He said nothin' about weird dance moves."

Brian glanced at his daughter and he smiled at her.

"Bassai Dai is hardly some funky dance moves. It was designed to penetrate a fortress." He walked over to the front door and the boy, who was taking a lick of his melting ice cream, watched him approach fearlessly. There was a hint of rebelliousness in his gaze. "Bassai Dai is a kata with some pretty important techniques and principles passed down from teacher to student. It teaches self-defence and so much more."

The boy licked his ice cream again. Kaylee could tell he was partially intrigued.

"Can anyone learn?" the boy asked. "The principles, I mean. And the self-defence stuff."

"With enough perseverance, effort and courage," her Dad said, "anything is possible.

Daniel Fellows is an author living and working in Perth, Western Australia. He is an avid and voracious reader; his main tastes are horror, sf, fantasy and thriller.

When he isn't writing and spending time with his wife and five children, he is driving dump trucks on an iron ore mine site in the Pilbara region of Western Australia. Daniel has a wide range of interests including playing bass guitar, learning German and reading history books.
.
A sample of books by Daniel J Fellows Available where all goood books are sold!

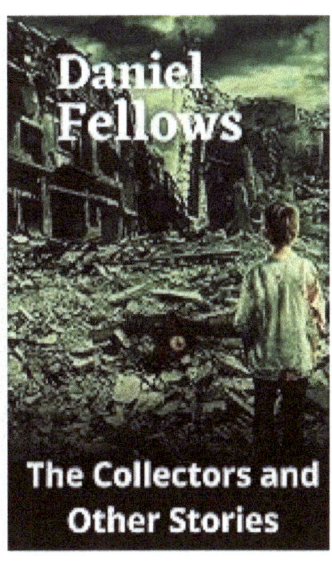

SOUTH WEST GOJU-RYU KARATE-DO ASSOCIATION INC (WA)

Female karate practitioners from the Peel, Bunbury-Geographe, and Perth regions gathered in the South West Goju Ryu Karate-Do Association's Mandurah dojo during the King's Birthday long weekend, for an empowering day of training, friendship, learning and skills development.

Highly-ranked female karate instructors representing a range of styles, including former state and national champions, led a group of 21 women and girls from 12 years of age at the fourth annual Women and Girls in Martial Arts Workshop.

SWGRKA's senior female students and instructors, Sempais Ann Draper and Shay Holdsworth of the Association's Mandurah dojo and Lisa Skrypichayko of the Bunbury dojo, organised the four-hour workshop. Along with Sensei Karen Hollings of Rei Shito-Ryu Karate, and Senseis Kim Benn and Marisa Simeone of KUA WA, they led sessions on a variety of subjects including self defence, kata, bo staff skills, speed and reflex drills, plus a special session about the importance of a positive mindset for girls and young women in martial arts.

The three participating karate clubs are supporters of Bunbury-based martial arts charity Pink Belt Project. Founder Kristy Hitchens says the annual Women in Martial Arts workshops actively demonstrate the benefits of martial arts for women.

"A big benefit reported by recipients of our Pink Belt Scholarships is the connection to community and sense of camaraderie provided by our Supporter Clubs," Kristy said. "This aspect was once again very much on display among workshop participants."

(L-R) Sensei Kim Benn - KUA WA Fremantle, Sensei Karen Hollings - Rei Shito-Ryu Karate Warnbro, Sempai Lisa Skrypichayko - SWGRKA Bunbury, Sempai Ann Draper - SWGRKA Mandurah, Sensei Marisa Simeone - KUA WA Fremantle, Sempai Shay Holdsworth - SWGRKA Mandurah

Kristy said there was a great deal of international research on the transformative effects of participation in the martial arts for women. "This is certainly reflected in the outcomes we are seeing through our mission of connecting women on a recovery journey to martial arts for healing, health, wellbeing and growth," she said. For more information about the Pink Belt Project, visit pinkbelt.com.au.

Sempai Ann Draper said female martial artists look forward each year to the workshop and its opportunities for girls and women across different styles of martial arts and levels of experience to connect with, challenge, and learn from one another.

"No matter our rank, age, or ability, martial arts are an important part of who we are and the friendships we make practicing together give us strength and courage." She said, adding, "Next year we will seek to include other styles of martial arts beyond karate."

SWGRKA's Chief Instructor Alan Burdett reported positive feedback on the workshop again this year, with participants praising the dynamic presentations and diverse topics covered.

"These seminars have become a highlight of our annual calendar - I'm pleased that female karateka from our Association are working with their colleagues from other styles to support each other in such a meaningful way," Hanshi Burdett added.

Visit the South West Goju Ryu Karate-Do Association's website at southwest-goju-karate.com, or email Chief Instructor Alan Burdett alan.burdett@email.com to learn more.

Write for Us

We want your authentic story, your journey and the reason WHY you love what you do. Below is a list of suggested topics. It is not exhaustive, so if you have an idea that we haven't come up with yet, drop us a line: training tips; technique workshops; style origins; kids in ma; training fuel; style anatomy; family pages; instructor profile; keeping it real; and more...

We are a quarterly magazine that celebrates and inspires a broad community of Martial Artists across the country. Our goal is to support all MA practitioners. Both instructors and students are encouraged to share their personal experiences, triumphs, and challenges within the style they love.

We feature interviews, rants, research, photography, projects and editorials that are respectful to all styles and are keeping in line with our magazine's inclusive philosophy.
Just as no two styles of Martial Arts are alike, our writers should have their own unique voice and tell their story from their own perspective. We encourage you to speak your truth.
Don't worry if you feel that your writing is not up to scratch, just tell us your story, your tip or your instruction the best way you can and our in-house editor will do the rest.

Email your submissions to info@martialartsmagazineaustralia.com
(text in .doc) and (photos in JPEG).

Our goal is to keep our magazine for the Martial Artists, not the profiteers. We will remain advertisement free, while endeavouring to produce a top-quality community magazine that we are all proud of. To keep sale costs low, we cannot offer contributors financial compensation for their submission. However, we will allow you to add your club and organisation's contact information to the footnote of your article along with your own bio and do our best to support and promote your style, book or cause through our social media and on our website.

In loving memory of Bruce.

Subscribe and Save
Visit
Martial Arts Magazine Australia

www.ingramcontent.com/pod-product-compliance
Lightning Source LLC
Chambersburg PA
CBHW061134010526
44107CB00068B/2939